Jurors' and Attorneys' Use of Social Media During Voir Dire, Trials, and Deliberations

A Report to the Judicial Conference Committee on Court Administration and Case Management

Meghan Dunn
Research Associate

Federal Judicial Center
May 1, 2014

This Federal Judicial Center publication was undertaken in furtherance of the Center's statutory mission to conduct and stimulate research and development for the improvement of judicial administration. While the Center regards the content as responsible and valuable, this publication does not reflect policy or recommendations of the Board of the Federal Judicial Center.

Executive Summary

At the request of the Judicial Conference Committee on Court Administration and Case Management (CACM), the Federal Judicial Center conducted a survey of district court judges to assess the frequency with which jurors used social media to communicate during trials and deliberations in the past two years, and to identify strategies for curbing this behavior. The survey also assessed the frequency with which attorneys use social media to conduct research on potential jurors during voir dire. The survey is a follow-up to one conducted in 2011 on jurors' use of social media; attorneys' use of social media was not addressed in the original survey. The results, based on the responses of 494 responding judges, indicate that detected social media use by jurors is infrequent and that most judges have taken steps to ensure jurors do not use social media in the courtroom. The most common strategies are using plain language to explain the reason behind the ban and incorporating social media use into jury instructions—either the model jury instructions provided by CACM or judges' own personal jury instructions. Judges admit that it is difficult to police jurors. Only 33 judges reported instances of detected social media use by jurors during trial or deliberations. Attorneys' use of social media to research prospective jurors during voir dire is difficult to detect and quantify; most judges do not know whether attorneys are accessing potential jurors' social media profiles during voir dire, and most judges do not address the issue with attorneys.

Use of Social Media in the Courtroom

CACM asked the Federal Judicial Center to develop and administer a short survey of district court judges on the use of social media in the courtroom. The survey was a follow-up to one conducted in 2011, and was designed to assess jurors' use of social media and to identify strategies judges have found to be effective and appropriate in curbing the use of social media by jurors. CACM was also interested in the frequency with which attorneys use social media to gather information about potential jurors during the voir dire process. Attorneys' use of social media was not addressed in the original 2011 survey. This report presents the findings from the follow-up survey.

Study Methods and Response Rate

In November 2013, we sent notice of the secure electronic questionnaire to all active and senior federal district judges. Two weeks later, we sent an email reminder to judges who had not yet responded. Of the 1,021 judges who received the questionnaire, 494 responded, for an overall response rate of 48%. The respondents represent all 94 districts as well as the Court of International Trade and the Court of Federal Claims. The respondents have a mean of 14.8 years on the bench, ranging from a few months to 50 years of service as a federal judge. Appendix A provides a breakdown of responding judges by district.

The online questionnaire allowed respondents to be routed automatically around questions that were not relevant to their situations; thus, judges answered different questions depending on their experiences. Because some judges were asked questions that other judges were not (e.g., about previous experience with social media use), and because not all judges responded to every question presented to them, the number of respondents varies across the questions. A copy of the questionnaire can be found at Appendix B.

Please keep in mind that the data from the survey represent judges' reported experiences and perceptions of jurors' and attorneys' use of social media. The data are not actual empirical measures of such behavior.

Incidence of Social Media Use by Jurors

The use of social media by jurors during trials and deliberations is still not a common occurrence, and has not increased in frequency over the past two years. Of the 494 judges who responded to the survey, only 33 judges (7%) reported any detectable instances of jurors using social media during the two years since the original survey(see Table 1). As shown below, the survey conducted in 2011 found only about 6% of the responding judges had detected any instance of jurors' social media use.

Table 1
Judges' Experience with Jurors Using Social Media to Communicate During a Trial or Deliberation

Have Jurors Used Social Media During Trial or Deliberations in the Past Two Years?	Judges selecting this option in 2013 ($n = 494$)		Judges selecting this option in 2011 ($n = 508$)	
	Number	Percentage	Number	Percentage
Yes	33	6.7	30	5.9
No	461	93.3	478	94.1

Of the 33 judges who have perceived juror use of social media, the majority (30 judges, or 97%) have seen social media use by a juror in only one or two cases. The instances of social media use were more commonly reported during trials (27 judges reported at least one instance) than deliberations (7 judges reported at least one instance), and were more commonly reported during criminal trials (21 judges with experience) than civil trials (8 judges). Two judges perceived jurors using social media during both criminal and civil trials.

Ways in Which Jurors Use Social Media

The forms of detected social media use by jurors include Facebook (17 responses), and instant messaging services (four responses). Twitter and personal blogs were reported by three judges. Table 2 contains a complete list of the social media forms judges perceived during trials and deliberations.

Table 2
Forms of Social Media During Trials and Deliberations

Social Media Forms	Judges selecting this option in 2013 (*n* = 28)[a]		Judges selecting this option in 2011 (*n* = 30)[a]	
	Number	Percentage	Number	Percentage
Facebook	17	60.7	9	30.0
Instant messaging service	4	14.3	7	23.3
Juror's personal blog	3	10.7	0	0.0
Twitter	3	10.7	3	10.0
Internet chat room	2	7.1	3	10.0

a. Judges could select more than one item; thus, the number of media forms identified is greater than the number of respondents.

A comparison with the 2011 survey shows that the social media forms used by jurors have changed—at least as reported by the judges—with more jurors using Facebook (9 judges, or 30%, in 2011) and personal blogs (0 instances in 2011), and fewer jurors using instant messaging services (7 judges, or 23%, in 2011). Detected usage of Twitter (3 judges, or 10%, in 2011) and Internet chat rooms (3 judges, or 10%, in 2011) has remained the same over the intervening two years. We cannot determine whether this is a true change in the social media used by jurors or a change in judges' ability to detect and recognize different types of social media used by jurors.

Of the 16 judges who described the type of social media use jurors engaged in, six judges reported that a juror divulged confidential information about the case (see Table 3). This is a change from the findings of the 2011 survey, in which no judge reported any instances of jurors using social media to divulge confidential information about a case. Additionally, three judges reported that a juror communicated or attempted to communicate directly with participants in the case, and two revealed aspects of the deliberation process. Judges could select "other" as an option for identifying additional ways in which jurors inappropriately used social media; the nine who did listed case-related research (five judges), sharing general jury-service information (three judges), and texting (one judge).

Table 3
Ways in Which Jurors Used Social Media During a Trial or Deliberation

Juror Behavior	Judges selecting this option in 2013 (*n* = 16)[a]		Judges selecting this option in 2011 (*n* = 17)[a]	
	Number	Percentage	Number	Percentage
Divulged confidential information about the case	6	37.5	0	0.0
Communicated or attempted to communicate directly with participants in the case (e.g., witnesses, parties, attorneys, judges)	3	18.8	3	17.6
Revealed aspects of the deliberation process	2	12.5	3	17.6
"Friended" or attempted to "friend" participants in the case (e.g., witnesses, parties, attorneys, judges)	1	6.3	3	17.6
Revealed identifying information about other jurors	0	0.0	1	5.9
Other	9	56.3	11	64.7

a. Judges could select more than one item; thus, the number of juror behaviors identified is greater than the number of respondents.

In an open-ended follow-up question, judges could describe more fully the ways in which jurors have used social media in their courtrooms. Overall, the 17 judges who responded to this question reported that jurors use social media to share generic information about jury service, and to conduct outside research. Of these 17 judges, five reported that jurors wrote about their jury service on Facebook. Three judges reported inappropriate outside research, either case-related (one judge) or to gather information about trial participants (two judges). Two judges reported jurors contacting trial participants, and only one reported a juror using social media to post about specific trial events. In the 2011 survey, judges reported that jurors had shared nonconfidential information about cases and information about jury service in general, as well as two situations in which jurors contacted parties with case-specific information during deliberations.

Identifying Jurors' Social Media Use During Trial and Deliberation

Judges acknowledge that it is difficult to detect jurors' inappropriate use of social media, and that judges rely on others to bring it to their attention. Of the 27 judges who indicated how they learned of the incident, 12 judges said another juror had reported it. Eight judges said an attorney had reported it, and seven said it was reported by court staff or by one of the parties. Three judges said a juror's use of social media came up in posttrial motions. Only one judge reported observing jurors using electronic devices in the courtroom.

Table 4
Ways in Which Judges Learned About Social Media Use by Jurors

Source of Social Media Detection	Judges selecting this option in 2013 (*n* = 27)[a]		Judges selecting this option in 2011 (*n* = 28)[a]	
	Number	Percentage	Number	Percentage
It was reported by another juror	12	44.4	13	46.4
It was reported by an attorney	8	29.6	5	17.9
It was reported by court staff	6	22.2	1	3.6
It was reported by one of the parties	1	3.7	1	3.6
I observed jurors using electronic devices in the courtroom	1	3.7	2	7.1
It arose during posttrial motions	3	11.1	5	17.9
Other	4	14.8	6	21.4

a. Judges could select more than one item; thus, the number of detection sources identified is greater than the number of respondents.

A comparison with the data from the 2011 survey suggests an increased awareness of the need to monitor jurors' use of social media; while jurors are still the most likely source of reporting (46% in 2011 and 44% in 2013), reporting by attorneys and court staff increased in the intervening two years.

When judges have learned of jurors using social media in their courtrooms, reactions have varied. Nineteen judges (70% of the 27 judges with experience) cautioned the juror, but allowed him or her to remain on the jury, and eight judges (30%) chose to remove the juror from the jury (see Table 5). A comparison with the data from the 2011 survey indicates that more judges are cautioning jurors (70% in 2013, compared with only 27% in 2011) and fewer are declaring mistrials (none in 2013, but 4 judges in 2011). Frequencies of other actions have remained essentially the same.

Table 5
Actions Taken by Judges When Social Media Use by a Juror Was Discovered

Action Taken	Judges selecting this option in 2013 (*n* = 27)[a]		Judges selecting this option in 2011 (*n* = 30)[a]	
	Number	Percentage	Number	Percentage
Cautioned juror, but allowed him or her to remain on jury	19	70.4	8	26.7
Removed juror from jury	8	29.6	9	30.0
Held juror in contempt of court	1	3.7	1	3.3
Fined juror	0	0.0	1	3.3
Declared a mistrial	0	0.0	4	13.3
Other	7	25.9	7	23.3

a.   Judges could select more than one item; thus, the number of actions identified is greater than the number of respondents.

A few judges reported that they dealt with the issue posttrial. In a free response section of the questionnaire, one judge reported he held a posttrial hearing to determine if the social media activity had any impact on the juror's performance of his or her duty. Two other judges reported that the instances were discovered after the trial had concluded; one of those judges considered the behavior in posttrial motion practice, the other could do nothing as the jurors had been released. These actions are similar to those reported in 2011, in which the four responding judges investigated the nature of the communication, either in posttrial hearings or by questioning the offending jurors directly.

Strategies for Preventing Jurors' Use of Social Media

The great majority of judges who responded have taken preventive measures to ensure that jurors do not use social media in their courtrooms (456 judges), with only 19 judges, or 4%, indicating that they have not specifically addressed jurors' use of social media. These numbers represent a slight decrease from the 2011 survey responses, in which 6% of responding judges, or 30 judges, had not specifically addressed social media use.

Judges were asked to identify steps they had taken to ensure that jurors did not use social media to communicate about a case. Table 6 shows the responses.

Table 6
Measure Taken to Ensure Jurors Do Not Use Social Media to Communicate

Preventive Measure	Judges selecting this option in 2013 ($n = 475$)[a]		Judges selecting this option in 2011 ($n = 508$)[a]	
	Number	Percentage	Number	Percentage
I have not specifically addressed jurors' use of social media	19	4.0	30	5.9
Explained, in plain language, the reason behind the social media ban	352	74.1	317	62.4
Instructed jurors at multiple points throughout the trial	334	70.3	271	53.3
Reminded jurors at voir dire to refrain from using social media while serving as a juror	257	54.1	199	39.2
Used the Judicial Conference Committee's model jury instructions before trial	251	52.8	262	51.2[b]
Used other jury instructions (i.e., not the model instructions) before trial	220	46.3	227	44.7
Used the Judicial Conference Committee's model jury instructions before deliberation	213	44.8	201	39.6[b]
Used other jury instruction (i.e., not the model instructions) before deliberation	164	34.5	176	34.6
Confiscated phones and other electronic devices during deliberation	143	30.1	147	28.9
Alerted the jury about the personal consequences	119	25.1	103	20.3
Confiscated phones and other electronic devices at the start of each day of trial	106	22.3	113	22.2
Required jurors to sign a statement of compliance or written pledge agreeing to refrain from using social media while serving as a juror	10	2.1	6	1.2

a. Judges could select more than one item; thus, the number of preventive measures identified is greater than the number of respondents.

b. In the 2011 survey, use of the model jury instructions was presented as a separate question.

The most common measure used by judges was to explain, in plain language, the reason behind the social media ban; 74% of the respondents to this question (or 352 judges) use this approach. The next most common approach, used by 70% of the judges (or 334 judges) was to instruct jurors at multiple points throughout the trial. Indeed, instructing the jury is very common. Some judges use

CACM's model jury instructions before trial (53%, or 251 judges) or before deliberation (45%, or 213 judges) and others use their own jury instructions before trial (46%, or 220 judges) or before deliberation (35%, or 164 judges). Fifteen judges provided copies of their social media jury instructions when they submitted their questionnaires. A compilation of those instructions can be found at Appendices C–Q.

Over half of the responding judges (54%, or 257 judges) remind jurors at voir dire to refrain from using social media while serving as a juror, and 25% (119 judges) alert the jury about the personal consequences of inappropriate social media use (i.e., individual fines or being held in contempt of court). Approximately one quarter of the responding judges reported confiscating cell phones and other electronic devices, with 22% (106 judges) doing so at the start of each day of trial and 30% (143 judges) doing so during deliberation. An additional 17 judges (39% of the 44 judges who provided a response) indicated, in a free response question, that their courthouse does not permit electronic devices or cell phones in the courtroom. Only 10 judges (2%) ask jurors to sign a statement of compliance agreeing to refrain from using social media while serving as a juror.

A comparison of the data from 2011 and 2013 shows that use of specific preventive measures has either increased or remained essentially the same over the two-year period. Judges' use of three measures increased by at least 11 percentage points: instructing jurors at multiple points throughout the trial (from 53% in 2011 to 70% in 2013); reminding jurors at voir dire to refrain from using social media (from 39% in 2011 to 54% in 2013); and explaining the reason behind the ban in plain language (from 62% in 2011 to 74% in 2013). The others either increased slightly in frequency (use of model jury instructions before deliberation, and alerting jurors about personal consequences) or did not change in frequency in the 2011 and 2013 surveys.

Other strategies for preventing jurors' use of social media include posting a notice in the jury assembly and deliberation rooms regarding the use of social media (ten judges, 23% of the 44 responding judges), administering a separate oath to jurors (four judges, or 9%), and asking jurors directly if they can or did comply with the ban on social media use (three judges, or 7%). One judge provided a copy of the oath with which jurors are asked to comply; that oath can be found at Appendix R.

As Table 7 shows, two-thirds of the responding judges (307, or 68%) reported their actions regarding social media to have been "very successful"; 29% (133 judges) said they did not know how successful their preventive measures have been.

Table 7
Success of Additional Preventive Measures for Social Media Use

Action Taken	Judges selecting this option in 2013 (*n* = 454)		Judges selecting this option in 2011 (*n* = 457)	
	Number	Percentage	Number	Percentage
Very successful	307	67.6	239	52.3
Somewhat successful	14	3.1	16	3.5
Not at all successful	0	0.0	0	0.0
I don't know	133	29.3	202	44.2

These numbers represent an increase from the 2011 survey, in which 52% of responding judges indicated that their actions regarding social media use were "very successful" and 44% said they did not know how successful their actions had been.

In an open-ended follow-up question that asked judges to explain the success of their preventive measures, the majority of responding judges (89% of the 228 judges who answered the question) indicated that they had no way of knowing if jurors have violated the social media prohibition but assumed full compliance. This represents an increase from 2011, in which 79% of the responding judges acknowledged they could not tell if jurors were using social media.

Twenty-six judges give repeated reminders about not communicating via social media, and 18 emphasize the importance of not allowing their decision to be based on outside information. Eleven judges stated in response to the survey that jurors take their jobs seriously and comply with the restrictions on social media use, and nine judges provide a plain English explanation for the prohibition. Five judges conduct post-verdict interviews with jurors to assess, among other things, the extent to which jurors comply with social media instructions, and three judges stated that prohibiting electronic devices or Internet connectivity in the courtroom makes it more difficult for jurors to use social media.

Eight judges described specific instances in which jurors used social media. Two judges reported jurors who conducted online research: one Googled definitions in the jury instructions, resulting in a mistrial, and the other looked up the defendant's name, resulting in that juror's dismissal. A third judge had a potential juror identify the defense counsel as being a Facebook friend, but not a close friend; the juror agreed to "unfriend" the attorney if selected. The remaining five judges did not specify how jurors used social media.

Additional Suggestions Regarding Social Media Use by Jurors

Judges were asked to suggest ways in which courts could prevent inappropriate use of social media by jurors during trial and deliberation. The most commonly cited suggestion, cited by 40% of the 331 judges who answered this question, was to give frequent reminders to jurors throughout the trial. There were nearly as many suggestions—36% of the 331 responding judges—to explain, in plain language, the reason behind the social media ban. Other suggestions included alerting jurors to personal and trial-related consequences of using social media (mentioned by 10% of responding judges), prohibiting cell phones and electronic devices (mentioned by 6% of responding judges), and posting notices and reminders in the jury room (mentioned by 3% of responding judges). Forty-one judges (or 12%) said no additional measures were required regarding jurors' use of social media.

Incidence of Social Media Use by Attorneys

The questionnaire also asked judges about their experiences with attorneys using social media in the courtroom during voir dire. Based on these responses, the incidence of attorneys' social media use is largely unknown. Of the 348 judges who responded to the question, 73%, or 255 judges, indicated they did not know the number of trials, if any, in which attorneys have used social media during voir dire. Twenty five judges (or 7% of those who responded) indicated they knew attorneys had used social media in at least one of their trials (see Table 8). Of the 25 judges who have seen attorneys use social media during voir dire, the majority (21 judges, or 84%) reported it to have occurred in five or fewer trials.

Table 8
Judges' Experience with Attorneys Using Social Media During Voir Dire

In How Many Trials Over Which You Have Presided Have Attorneys Used Social Media During Voir Dire?	Judges selecting this option ($n = 348$)	
	Number	Percentage
I don't know	255	73.3
Between 1 and 5	21	6.0
Between 6 and 10	2	0.6
Between 11 and 20	2	0.6
More than 20	0	0.0
None	68	19.5

Judges' inability to tell whether attorneys were using social media makes it difficult to assess in what types of trials it is most frequently used. The majority of judges (90% of the 303 who responded to the question) indicated they did not know in what types of trial attorneys were using social media during voir dire. Twelve judges indicated that attorneys used social media during voir dire in both criminal and civil trials, whereas 11 judges reported it in criminal trials and eight in civil trials.

Ways in Which Attorneys Used Social Media

The forms of social media attorneys reportedly used during voir dire included looking at prospective jurors' Facebook pages (15 responses), running prospective jurors' names through Google or another search engine (15 responses), and looking at prospective jurors' LinkedIn profiles or personal blogs and websites (8 responses each). Again, however, the majority of responding judges (90%, or 298 of the 329 responding judges) indicated that they did not know what forms of social media attorneys were using, if any. Because the judges were responding to a pre-set list of options, they may have simply checked those they thought most likely. Table 9 contains a complete list of social media forms used by attorneys.

Table 9
Forms of Social Media Used by Attorneys

Forms of Social Media	Judges selecting this option $(n = 329)^a$	
	Number	Percentage
Don't know	298	90.6
Looking at prospective jurors' Facebook pages	15	4.6
Running prospective jurors' names through Google or other search engine	15	4.6
Looking at prospective jurors' LinkedIn profile	8	2.4
Looking at prospective jurors' personal blogs or websites	8	2.4
Looking at prospective jurors' Twitter accounts	6	1.8

a. Judges could select more than one item; thus, the number of media forms identified is greater than the number of respondents.

Judges Rules About Attorneys' Use of Social Media During Voir Dire

Not all judges specifically address the issue of attorneys' use of social media to research prospective jurors during voir dire (see Table 10). Only 31% of the 466 responding judges reported doing so, with 120 judges forbidding attorneys to research prospective jurors using social media during voir dire (26% of responding judges) and only 23 judges directly allowing it.

Table 10
Judges' Permission for Attorneys to Use Social Media

Do You Permit Attorneys to Use Social Media During Voir Dire?	Judges selecting this option $(n = 466)$	
	Number	Percentage
Yes	23	4.9
No	120	25.8
I don't address this issue with attorneys before voir dire	323	69.3

A follow-up free response question asked judges who do not permit attorneys to use social media during voir dire to explain why they forbid it. Overall, the responses indicate both privacy concerns for the jurors and logistical considerations. Of the 89 judges who answered the question, almost 20% (or 17 judges) indicated they did not allow attorneys to research prospective jurors during voir dire in order to protect the jurors' privacy, and 4 judges (4%) were worried about intimidating potential jurors. Other judges thought such activity would be too distracting (15 judges, or 17%), or that this type of research would prolong voir dire (14 judges, or 16%). One-third of responding judges (19 judges) indicated that attorneys using social media to research jurors during voir dire was unnecessary, either because attorneys are able to conduct that research before they arrive at court if they so choose (9 judges) or because the information provided during voir dire is sufficient (10 judges). Judges also worried about the potential effects of attorneys' actions; five judges noted that allowing attorneys to research potential jurors during voir dire may create an unfair advantage for one side, and four of the responding judges prohibited such research because there is no way to evaluate the accuracy of the information gathered. Eleven judges said they had never been asked by attorneys.

When judges do permit attorneys to use social media to research potential jurors during voir dire, most (62%, or 204 judges) do not require the attorneys to share that information with the court or other attorneys (see Table 11). Five of the responding judges (or 2% of the 330 who answered this question) reported they require attorneys to share information on potential jurors with both the court and other attorneys; only one judge required that the information be shared only with the court. Over one-third of responding judges, however, do not know whether such information is shared with other attorneys.

Table 11
Requirements About Sharing Social Media Results

Do Attorneys Have to Share Information Obtained Via Social Media?	Judges selecting this option (*n* = 330)	
	Number	Percentage
No	204	61.8
Yes, with both the court and other attorneys	5	1.5
Yes, with the court	1	0.3
Yes, with other attorneys	0	0.0
I don't know	120	36.4

Judges were also asked whether they disclosed to the venire panel that attorneys may be looking at their social media accounts. Most judges (315 of the 336 who responded) reported they do not disclose that information to potential jurors; only eight judges (2%) reported doing so.

Attorneys' Inappropriate Use of Social Media

Judges did not report many problems with attorneys using social media, either during voir dire or in other stages of a trial. When asked about attorneys' actions during voir dire, only three judges (5% of the 64 responding judges) indicated experience with an attorney who followed a prospective juror on Twitter. No judges reported attorneys "friending" or attempting to "friend" a prospective juror on Facebook (e.g., to get past privacy settings) or subscribing to a prospective juror's personal blog. In an open-ended follow-up question, judges could describe more fully the ways in which attorneys used social media. Of the 58 judges who did so, none reported negative experiences with attorneys using social media.

In a free response section of the questionnaire, judges were asked to describe any other problems they may have encountered with social media use by attorneys, either in voir dire or other stages of a case. Three judges described situations in which social media was a factor. One judge noted that an attorney followed a juror's posting after the trial was completed and used those posts to challenge the verdict. Another judge indicated that information transmitted via social media has been used as the basis for a supervised release violation. A third judge referenced *United States v. Bowen*, in which convictions were overturned as a result of online prosecutorial misconduct.

Five judges noted that attorneys in their courtrooms were unable to use social media, either because of the time constraints of voir dire (four judges) or because of the court's prohibition of electronics in the courtroom (one judge). Four judges admitted that their focus is more on the use of social media by jurors and less on attorneys' actions concerning social media.

Summary

The detected use of social media by jurors during trials and deliberations is not common, but does occur. Thirty-three out of the 494 judges who responded reported instances in which jurors were detected using social media, most often during criminal cases. Social media use most often took the form of revealing confidential information about a case. There were several instances of jurors attempting to contact participants in the case via social media. When social media use was detected, it was most likely to be reported by a fellow juror.

Although the overall incidence of detected social media use by jurors has remained the same in the two years since the original survey was conducted, the specifics of what jurors are communicating has changed, with an increase in the divulgence of confidential case information.

Judges are aware that some jurors are using social media and have taken steps to address its use in the courtroom. The majority of judges have taken at least some precautionary steps to ensure that jurors do not use social media in their courtroom. The most common strategy is explaining to the jury in plain language the reason behind the social media ban, followed closely by incorporating social media use into their jury instructions and reminding jurors at voir dire to refrain from using social media. Judges admit that it is difficult to police jurors, making it hard to evaluate frequency and assess the impact of preventive measures.

Attorneys' use of social media to research prospective jurors during voir dire is difficult to both detect and quantify; most judges do not know whether attorneys are accessing potential jurors' social media profiles during voir dire, and most do not address the issue with attorneys.

Appendix A
Responding Judges by District

		Frequency	Percent	Valid Percent	Cumulative Percent
Valid	AK	1	.2	.2	.2
	ALM	3	.6	.6	.8
	ALN	7	1.4	1.4	2.2
	ALS	3	.6	.6	2.8
	AO	1	.2	.2	3.0
	ARE	4	.8	.8	3.9
	ARW	1	.2	.2	4.1
	AZ	11	2.2	2.2	6.3
	CAC	13	2.6	2.6	8.9
	CAE	8	1.6	1.6	10.5
	CAN	7	1.4	1.4	12.0
	CAS	8	1.6	1.6	13.6
	CO	8	1.6	1.6	15.2
	CT	5	1.0	1.0	16.2
	Ct of Fed Claims	2	.4	.4	16.6
	Ct of Intl Trade	5	1.0	1.0	17.6
	DC	8	1.6	1.6	19.3
	DE	2	.4	.4	19.7
	FLM	11	2.2	2.2	21.9
	FLN	5	1.0	1.0	22.9
	FLS	6	1.2	1.2	24.1
	GAM	4	.8	.8	24.9
	GAN	5	1.0	1.0	26.0
	GAS	1	.2	.2	26.2
	GU	1	.2	.2	26.4
	HI	2	.4	.4	26.8
	IAN	3	.6	.6	27.4
	IAS	5	1.0	1.0	28.4
	ID	2	.4	.4	28.8
	ILC	4	.8	.8	29.6
	ILN	16	3.2	3.2	32.9

ILS	2	.4	.4	33.3
INN	4	.8	.8	34.1
INS	4	.8	.8	34.9
KS	4	.8	.8	35.7
KYE	5	1.0	1.0	36.7
KYW	2	.4	.4	37.1
LAE	6	1.2	1.2	38.3
LAM	2	.4	.4	38.7
LAW	6	1.2	1.2	40.0
MA	8	1.6	1.6	41.6
MD	12	2.4	2.4	44.0
ME	4	.8	.8	44.8
MIE	11	2.2	2.2	47.1
MIW	5	1.0	1.0	48.1
MN	6	1.2	1.2	49.3
MOE	5	1.0	1.0	50.3
MOW	5	1.0	1.0	51.3
MSN	2	.4	.4	51.7
MSS	4	.8	.8	52.5
MT	2	.4	.4	52.9
NCE	4	.8	.8	53.8
NCM	2	.4	.4	54.2
NCW	2	.4	.4	54.6
ND	2	.4	.4	55.0
NE	5	1.0	1.0	56.0
NH	1	.2	.2	56.2
NJ	8	1.6	1.6	57.8
NM	6	1.2	1.2	59.0
NMI	1	.2	.2	59.2
NV	4	.8	.8	60.0
NYE	12	2.4	2.4	62.5
NYN	5	1.0	1.0	63.5
NYS	14	2.8	2.8	66.3
NYW	3	.6	.6	66.9
OHN	10	2.0	2.0	69.0

OHS	8	1.6	1.6	70.6
OKE	1	.2	.2	70.8
OKN	4	.8	.8	71.6
OKW	6	1.2	1.2	72.8
OR	6	1.2	1.2	74.0
PAE	13	2.6	2.6	76.7
PAM	9	1.8	1.8	78.5
PAW	9	1.8	1.8	80.3
PR	4	.8	.8	81.1
RI	1	.2	.2	81.3
SC	10	2.0	2.0	83.4
SD	3	.6	.6	84.0
TNE	3	.6	.6	84.6
TNM	3	.6	.6	85.2
TNW	3	.6	.6	85.8
TXE	5	1.0	1.0	86.8
TXN	5	1.0	1.0	87.8
TXS	9	1.8	1.8	89.7
TXW	10	2.0	2.0	91.7
UT	3	.6	.6	92.3
VAE	8	1.6	1.6	93.9
VAW	5	1.0	1.0	94.9
VI	1	.2	.2	95.1
VT	1	.2	.2	95.3
WAE	6	1.2	1.2	96.6
WAW	6	1.2	1.2	97.8
WIE	2	.4	.4	98.2
WIW	1	.2	.2	98.4
WVN	3	.6	.6	99.0
WVS	4	.8	.8	99.8
WY	1	.2	.2	100.0
Total	493	100.0	100.0	

Appendix B
Survey Document

Use of Social Media in Courtrooms

This survey seeks (1) to assess the frequency with which jurors are using social media to communicate about cases during trial and deliberation, (2) to identify strategies judges have found to be effective and appropriate in curbing this behavior, and (3) to assess the frequency with which courts are permitting attorneys to use social media during voir dire. For the purposes of this survey, social media is defined as electronic communications, usually internet-based, through which users create online communities to share ideas, personal messages and other content. It includes, but is not limited to, social networking sites such as Facebook, Twitter, LinkedIn and YouTube, as well as platforms such as blogs, chatrooms and online bulletin boards.

For the purposes of this survey, please focus on jurors' use of social media to communicate information about cases, and attorneys' use of social media to research prospective jurors. At this point, we are not considering instances of jurors' use of the internet to conduct independent research about the case.

A. Experience with Social Media Use by Jurors

1. In the past two years, have you experienced any instances of jurors using social media to communicate during a trial or deliberations?
- ○ Yes
- ○ No

2. In how many trials and/or deliberations in the past two years have you encountered jurors using social media to communicate?
- ○ 1-2
- ○ 3-5
- ○ 6-10
- ○ More than 10

3. Approximately how many of these instances were during a trial?

4. Approximately how many of these instances were during deliberations?

5. In what types of cases did you encounter jurors using social media to communicate?
- ○ Criminal trials
- ○ Civil trials
- ○ Both criminal and civil trials

6. Which of the following forms of social media have jurors used to communicate trial or deliberation information about your courtroom or about cases in which you have presided? Please check all that apply.
- ❑ Twitter
- ❑ Facebook
- ❑ LinkedIn
- ❑ Instagram
- ❑ Tumblr
- ❑ Instant messaging service (such as AIM)
- ❑ Juror's personal blog
- ❑ Internet bulletin board/forum
- ❑ Internet chat room
- ❑ Other (please specify) _____

7. How did you discover that a particular juror was using social media to communicate about a case? Please check all that apply.

❑ It was reported by another juror
❑ It was reported by an attorney
❑ It was reported by court staff
❑ It was reported by one of the parties
❑ I observed jurors using electronic devices in the courtroom
❑ It arose during post-trial motions
❑ Other (please specify) _____

8. To the best of your knowledge, have jurors in any of your cases used social media to do any of the following? Please check all that apply.

❑ "Friended" or attempted to "friend" participants in the case (e.g., witnesses, parties, other jurors, attorneys, judges)
❑ Communicated or attempted to communicate directly with participants in the case (e.g., witnesses, parties, other jurors, attorneys, judges)
❑ Divulged confidential information about the case
❑ Revealed aspects of the deliberation process
❑ Revealed identifying information about other jurors
❑ Other (please specify) _____

9. Please use the space below to describe more fully the way(s) in which jurors have used social media to communicate during trials and deliberations.

10. When you have found jurors using social media during trial or deliberation, what action(s) have you taken? Please check all that apply.

❑ Removed juror from jury
❑ Cautioned juror, but allowed him or her to remain on jury
❑ Fined juror
❑ Held juror in contempt of court
❑ Declared a mistrial
❑ Other (please specify) _____

B. Measures Taken to Prevent Jurors from Using Social Media

11. What actions have you taken to ensure that jurors do not use social media to communicate about the case during trial or deliberations? Please check all that apply.

❑ I have not specifically addressed jurors' use of social media.

❑ Used the Judicial Conference Committee's model jury instructions before trial

❑ Used the Judicial Conference Committee's model jury instructions before deliberation

❑ Used other jury instructions (i.e., not the model instructions) before trial

❑ Used other jury instructions (i.e., not the model instructions) before deliberation

❑ Instructed jurors at multiple points throughout the trial (i.e., at the end of each day of testimony)

❑ Confiscated phones and other electronic devices at the start of each day of trial

❑ Confiscated phones and other electronic devices during deliberation

❑ Explained, in plain language, the reason behind the social media ban

❑ Alerted the jury about the personal consequences (i.e., personal fines, contempt of court)

❑ Reminded jurors at voir dire to refrain from using social media while serving as a juror

❑ Required jurors to sign a statement of compliance or written pledge agreeing to refrain from using social media while serving as a juror

❑ Other (please specify) _____

12. If you use or have used a set of instructions other than the Judicial Conference Committee's model jury instructions during a trial or deliberations, please attach those instructions below, or email the text of those instructions to socialmediasurvey@fjc.gov.

13. How successful have these actions been?

○ Very successful

○ Somewhat successful

○ Not at all successful

○ I don't know

14. Please explain.

15. What suggestions do you have for steps judges or courts can take to prevent inappropriate use of social media by jurors? Please be as detailed as possible.

C. Attorneys' Use of Social Media During Voir Dire

16. Do you permit attorneys in your courtroom to use social media to research prospective jurors during the voir dire process?
- ○ Yes
- ○ No
- ○ I don't address this issue with attorneys before voir dire

17. Why do you not permit attorneys to use social media during voir dire?

18. In how many trials over which you have presided have attorneys used social media during voir dire?
- ○ 1-5
- ○ 6-10
- ○ 11-20
- ○ More than 20
- ○ I don't know
- ○ None

19. In what type of trial did attorneys use social media during voir dire?
- ○ Criminal trials
- ○ Civil trials
- ○ Both criminal and civil trials
- ○ I don't know

20. In which of the following ways do attorneys in your courtroom use social media during voir dire? Please check all that apply.
- ❑ Looking at prospective jurors' Facebook pages
- ❑ Looking at prospective jurors' Twitter accounts
- ❑ Looking at prospective jurors' LinkedIn profiles
- ❑ Looking at prospective jurors' personal blogs or websites
- ❑ Running prospective jurors' names through Google or other search engines
- ❑ Don't know
- ❑ Other, please specify _____

21. What, if any, guidelines do you give to attorneys using social media during voir dire?

22. Do attorneys have to share information about potential jurors obtained via social media with the court or other attorneys?
- ○ Yes, with the court
- ○ Yes, with other attorneys
- ○ Yes, with both the court and other attorneys
- ○ No
- ○ I don't know

23. Do you disclose to the venire panel that attorneys may be looking at their social media accounts during voir dire?

O Yes

O No

O It depends (please specify) _____

24. To the best of your knowledge, have attorneys in any of your cases used social media to do any of the following? Please check all that apply.

❑ "Friended" or attempted to "friend" a prospective juror on Facebook to get past privacy settings

❑ Followed a prospective juror on Twitter

❑ Subscribed to a prospective juror's personal blog

❑ Other, please specify. _____

25. Have you encountered any other problems regarding social media use by attorneys, either in voir dire or in other aspects of a case?

D. Demographic Information

26. What is your home district?

27. For how many years have you served as a federal judge?

28. Do you have any experience, either as a judge in the state system, or as a practitioner in the federal or state systems, with the issues involved in this survey? If so, please share and be as detailed as possible.

29. If you have any additional comments about jurors' or attorneys' use of social media in general, please provide them here.

Thank you for completing the survey. Please click the "Submit Survey" button below to submit your responses. If you have any questions about the survey, please contact Meghan Dunn at mdunn@fjc.gov or 805-226-7497.

Appendix C
Jury Instructions from Judge Richard G. Kopf (D. Neb.)

Preliminary Jury Instructions for Use in Criminal Cases
Introduction

Ladies and gentlemen: I will take a few moments now to give you some initial instructions about this case and about your duties as jurors. At the end of the trial I will give you further instructions. I may also give you instructions during the trial. Unless I specifically tell you otherwise, all such instructions - both those I give you now and those I give you later - are equally binding on you and must be followed.

Serving as a Juror on this Criminal Case

This is a criminal case, brought against the defendant[s] by the United States government. You should understand that the government's charges are simply accusations. They are not evidence of anything. The defendant[s] [has] [have] pleaded not guilty, and [is] [are] presumed to be innocent unless and until proved guilty beyond a reasonable doubt to the unanimous satisfaction of all the members of the jury.

It will be your duty to decide from the evidence whether [the] [each] defendant is guilty or not guilty of the crime[s] charged. From the evidence, you will decide what the facts are. You are entitled to consider that evidence in the light of your own observations and experiences in the affairs of life. You may use reason and common sense to draw deductions or conclusions from facts which have been established by the evidence. You will then apply those facts to the law which I give you in these and in my other instructions, and in that way reach your verdict. You are the sole judges of the facts; but you must follow the law as stated in my instructions, whether you agree with it or not.

Please remember that only [this defendant] [these defendants], not anyone else, [is] [are] on trial here, and that [this defendant] [these defendants] [is] [are] on trial only for the crime[s] charged and not for anything else.

Elements of the Offense

In order to help you follow the evidence, I will now give you a brief summary of the elements of the crime[s] charged, which the government must prove beyond a reasonable doubt to make its case. Please refer to Exhibit A which is attached to these instructions. I will read Exhibit A to you at this time.

You should understand, however, that what I have just given you is only a preliminary outline. At the end of the trial I will give you final instructions on these matters. If there is any difference between what I just told you, and what I tell you in the instructions I give you at the end of the trial, the instructions given at the end of the trial must govern you.

What Testimony to Believe

In deciding what the facts are, you may have to decide what testimony you believe and what testimony you do not believe. You may believe all of what a witness says, or only part of it, or none of it.

In deciding what testimony to believe, consider the witnesses' intelligence, their opportunity to have seen or heard the things they testify about, their memories, any motives they may have for testifying a certain way, their manner while testifying, whether they said something different at an earlier time, the general reasonableness of their testimony and the extent to which their testimony is consistent with other evidence that you believe.

No Sympathy or Prejudice

Do not allow sympathy or prejudice to influence you. The law demands of you a just verdict, unaffected by anything except the evidence, your common sense, and the law as I give it to you. You should not take anything I may say or do during the trial as indicating what I think of the evidence or what I think your verdict should be.

What Is and Is Not Evidence

I have mentioned the word "evidence." "Evidence" includes the testimony of witnesses; documents and other things received as exhibits; any facts that have been stipulated, that is, formally agreed to by the parties; and any facts that have been judicially noticed--that is facts which I say you may accept as true.

    Certain things are not evidence. I will list those things for you now:

    1. Statements, arguments, questions and comments by lawyers are not evidence.

    2. Objections are not evidence. Lawyers have a right to object when they believe something is improper. You should not be influenced by the objection. If I sustain an objection to a question, you must ignore the question and must not try to guess what the answer might have been.

    3. Testimony that I strike from the record, or tell you to disregard, is not evidence and must not be considered.

    4. Anything you see or hear about this case outside the courtroom is not evidence, unlessI specifically tell you otherwise during the trial.

    5. Exhibits that are identified by a party but not received in evidence are not evidence.

    Furthermore, a particular item of evidence is sometimes received for a limited purpose only. That is, it can be used by you only for one particular purpose, and not for any other purpose. I will tell you when that occurs, and instruct you on the purposes for which the item can and cannot be used. You should also pay particularly close attention to such an instruction, because it may not be available to you in writing later in the jury room.

    Some of you may have heard the terms "direct evidence" and "circumstantial evidence." You should not be concerned with those terms. The federal law makes no distinction between the weight to be given to direct and circumstantial evidence.

No Transcript Available But Note-Taking Allowed

At the end of the trial you must make your decision based on what you recall of the evidence. You will not have a written transcript to consult, and it is not feasible to play back lengthy testimony. You must pay close attention to the testimony as it is given.

    If you wish, however, you may take notes to help you remember what witnesses said. If you do take notes, please keep them to yourself until you and your fellow jurors go to the jury room to decide the case. Do not let note-taking distract you so that you do not hear other answers by the witness. When you leave at night, your notes will be secured and not read by anyone.

Jurors Not Allowed to Question Witnesses

I do not permit jurors to ask questions of a witness whether orally or in writing. Moreover, I do not allow jurors to give me a question for presentation to the witness. In other words, you will not be allowed to question witnesses directly or indirectly.

Conduct of the Jury

You must strictly obey the following rules during all recesses and throughout the trial: First, do not talk among yourselves about this case, or about anyone involved with it, until the end of the case when you go to the jury room to decide on your verdict.

Second, do not talk or correspond with anyone else about this case, or about anyone involved with it, until the trial has ended and you have been discharged as jurors. In particular, do not "blog, tweet or twitter" or post anything on "My Space," "Facebook" or "You Tube" or similar sites about this case or about your service as a juror until this trial has ended and you have been discharged as jurors.

Third, when you are outside the courtroom, do not let anyone tell you anything about the case, or about anyone involved with it. If someone should try to talk to you about the case please report it to me.

Fourth, during the trial you should not talk with or speak to any of the parties, lawyers or witnesses involved in this case--you should not even pass the time of day with any of them.

Fifth, if there is news coverage of this case, do not read any news stories or articles about the case, or about anyone involved with it, or listen to any radio or television reports about the case or about anyone involved with it.

Sixth, do not do any research or make any investigation about the case on your own. Do not conduct research on the Internet about this case or about anyone involved with it. Do not consult any books such as dictionaries or similar references about this case or about anyone involved with it.

Seventh, do not make up your mind during the trial about what the verdict should be. On the contrary, keep an open mind until after you have gone to the jury room to decide the case and you and your fellow jurors have discussed the evidence.

Eighth, if you need to communicate with me do so only in writing by giving the courtroom deputy a note which is signed by you and dated. Please do not ask the courtroom deputy questions about the law or the evidence. The courtroom deputy is not allowed to answer such questions.

Richard G. Kopf
United States District Judge

Appendix D
Jury Instructions from Judge Jane E. Magnus-Stinson (S.D. Ind.)

Preliminary Instruction No. 14

All jurors must follow certain rules of conduct, and you must follow them, too.

First, until you are discharged as a juror, you must not consume any alcohol, drugs, or other substances that would prevent you from understanding and considering the evidence in this case fairly and impartially.

Second, until you have finished your deliberations, you must not discuss this case with anyone—including with members of your family, people involved in the trial, or anyone else. This includes not mentioning this case on Facebook, Twitter, MySpace, on a blog, or on a post to any website. You must not let others discuss the case with you. If anyone tries to talk to you about the case please let me know about it immediately. The trial lawyers are not allowed to speak with you during this case. When you see them at recess or pass them in the halls and they do not speak to you, they are not being rude or unfriendly; they are simply following the law. If any attempt is made by anyone to talk to you concerning this case, you should report that fact to the Courtroom Deputy immediately.

Third, you must decide this case based solely on the evidence presented here within the four walls of this courtroom. This means that during the trial you must not conduct any independent research about this case, the matters in the case, and the individuals or corporations involved in the case. In other words, you should not consult dictionaries or reference materials, search the internet, websites, blogs, or use any other electronic tools to obtain information about this case or to help you decide the case. Please do not try to find out information from any source outside the confines of this courtroom.

Fourth, you must not read any news stories or articles or listen to any radio or television reports about the case or about anyone who has anything to do with it.

Fifth, if you need to communicate with me, you must give a signed note to the bailiff to give to me.

Sixth, you must not make up your mind about what the verdict should be until after you have gone to the jury room to decide the case and you and your fellow jurors have discussed the evidence. Until that time, do not discuss the case with your fellow jurors, and keep an open mind.

Finally, if at any time you decide that you have personal knowledge about any fact that is material to this case, you must inform the Court immediately in writing.

Final Instruction No. 12

Once you start deliberating, do not communicate about the case or your deliberations with anyone except other members of your jury. You may not communicate with others about the case or your deliberations by any means. This includes oral or written communication, as well as any electronic method of communication, such as [list current technology or services likely to be used, e.g., telephone, cell phone, smart phone, iPhone, Blackberry, computer, text messaging, instant messaging, the Internet, chat rooms, blogs, websites, or services like Facebook, MySpace, LinkedIn, YouTube, Twitter], or any other method of communication.

If you need to communicate with me while you are deliberating, send a note through the bailiff. The note should be signed by the presiding juror, or by one or more members of the jury. To have a complete record of this trial, it is important that you do not communicate with me except by a written note. I may have to talk to the lawyers about your message, so it may take me some time to get back to you. You may continue your deliberations while you wait for my answer. Often the Court cannot answer a question except by re-reading the jury instructions, so you may find an answer to any question you have in the instructions. Please be advised that transcripts of trial testimony are not available to you. You must rely on your collective memory of the testimony.

If you send me a message, do not include the breakdown of any votes you may have conducted. In other words, do not tell me that you are split 6–6, or 8–4, or whatever your vote happens to be.

Appendix E
Jury Instructions from Judge Katherine Polk Failla (S.D.N.Y.)

Function of the jury

Before we go any further, let me explain a few basic rules of law that must guide all of us during this trial. The function of the jury is to decide questions of fact. Those of you who are chosen as jurors will be the only judges of the facts and nothing the Court or the lawyers say or do may in any way intrude on your role as the exclusive fact-finders, based only on the evidence presented. When it comes to the law, as distinguished from the facts, however, you must take your instructions from the Court — that is, from me —and you are bound by those instructions. You may not substitute your own ideas of what the law is or what you think the law should be. At the conclusion of the case, your job will be to determine whether the Government has proven, beyond a reasonable doubt, that Defendant Rudolph Bartee is guilty of the crimes charged.

Let me add that, during the course of the trial, you will receive all the evidence that you properly may consider to decide the case. Because of this, unless and until you are excused as a juror, you should not attempt to gather any information on your own relating to the case. Do not engage in any outside reading on this case. Do not attempt to visit any places mentioned in the case. Do not use the internet — Google, Facebook, Twitter or any other social media site — to learn anything about the case or anyone involved in the case. Do not do research of any nature or talk to anyone about the facts of the case or anyone involved in it. The reason for these rules, as I am certain you understand, is that your decision in this case must be made solely on the evidence presented at trial.

Our purpose, as I am sure you know, is to make sure that we have a jury of citizens who will decide the issues in this case both fairly and impartially, and without any bias or prejudice in favor of, or against, either side; and who will decide the case based solely on the evidence that is presented in court during the trial. In order to do that, I am going to ask certain questions of you — questions about your personal background, your family, some of your beliefs and attitudes about certain matters, how you are employed, and so forth.

It is very important that your answers to the questions posed be complete and truthful. Although the questions may cover many areas, it is your duty to honestly and conscientiously answer them, and to make your answers as full and complete as possible. False or misleading answers may result in the seating of a juror who might have been discharged by the Court for cause, or stricken by a party's exercise of a peremptory challenge, and thus could result in a miscarriage of justice.

You should understand that my questioning is not intended to pry into your lives, but to make sure that we select fair and impartial jurors, who can listen to the evidence with an open mind, and decide the issues in this case based only on the sworn testimony given in this courtroom, on whatever exhibits may be received in evidence, and on my instructions as to the law.

From your answers to my questions, I will be able to determine whether you should be excused "for cause" — that means, for a good reason. Your answers will also allow the lawyers to make intelligent use of their peremptory challenges. Peremptory challenges give each party the right to excuse a certain number of jurors without giving any reason for doing so.

If you are excused from serving as a juror in this case, you will get your jury card from Mr. Lopez and return to the jury assembly room where you will likely be sent to another courtroom to go through the same process in a different matter. If you are excused, do not consider that a reflection on you personally. This is all part of our system of justice, which is intended to provide all parties with a fair and impartial jury. You will have done your duty by your presence and your readiness to serve if chosen.

My questions to you, and your answers to them, are not evidence in this case, and you should not regard them as having any bearing in this case. That being said, it is very important that you not say in open court anything about the parties in this case or about any other matter that might affect the open- mindedness and fairness of other jurors. If there are any matters that you feel should be disclosed to me that might influence the other jurors or that you feel uncomfortable sharing in front of others for that matter, you should ask to approach the bench to discuss them at the appropriate time.

We will be selecting twelve jurors and two alternate jurors. Alternate jurors will be on standby, ready to take the place of a juror, should the circumstances require. Unless an alternate juror is asked to take the place of a juror, the alternate jurors will not participate in the jury's deliberations.

Preliminary Instructions to the Jury
Rules of Conduct

Finally, let me caution you about certain rules and principles governing your conduct as jurors in this case. First, you must not talk to each other about this case or about anyone who has anything to do with it until the end of the case when you go to the jury room to decide on your verdict. The reason for this requirement is that you must not reach any conclusion on the claims or defenses until all of the evidence is in. As I have said, keep an open mind until you start your deliberations at the end of the case.

Second, do not communicate with anyone else about this case or with anyone who has anything to do with it until the trial has ended and you have been discharged as jurors. Anyone else includes members of your family and your friends. And no communicating about the case means no communicating on Facebook, Twitter, blogs, whatever. You may tell your family and friends that you are a juror in a criminal case, but please do not tell them anything else about it until you have been discharged by me.

Third, do not let anyone talk to you about the case or about anyone who has anything to do with it. If any person should attempt to communicate with you about this case at any time throughout the trial, either in or out of the courthouse, you must immediately report that to my Deputy, Mr. Lopez, and to no one else. When I say report that communication to no one else, I mean that you should not tell anyone, including your fellow jurors.

To minimize the probability of any such improper communication, it is important that you go straight to the jury room when you come in in the morning and that you remain in the jury room for the duration of the trial day. You should use the bathrooms in the jury room rather than the bathrooms on this or any other floor; as you were probably told already, you may not use the cafeteria; and you must not use the public telephone on this floor. Given that our morning and afternoon breaks will be short, it is best that you remain in the jury room if you can.

Fourth, do not do any research or any investigation about the case or about anyone who has anything to with the case on your own. Don't go visit any place described in the trial. Don't read or listen to or watch any news reports about the case, if there are any. Don't go on the Internet or use whatever digital or communications device it is you use to see what you can learn to inform yourself about this matter.

That is because your decision in this case must be made solely on the evidence presented at the trial. In other words, all that you need to know will be presented here in open court by the very capable counsel who represent the parties. I expect you to inform me immediately through Mr. Lopez if you become aware of another juror's violation of these instructions.

Finally, each of you has been given a notebook and pen. That is because I permit jurors to take notes. But you do not have to take notes. Notes are just an aid to your own recollection. The court reporters in this case record everything that is said in the courtroom and any portion of the testimony can be read back to you during your deliberations. If you do take notes, be aware that note-taking may distract you from something important that is happening on the witness stand. Also, if you do take notes, please begin writing on the second page of your legal pad, and please put your juror number on the first page of the pad, so that we can be sure that only you will be making and reviewing the notes that are written in your pad

I want to emphasize that your notes are not to be shared with fellow jurors during deliberations, that the fact that a juror has taken notes will not entitle him or her to any greater voice in the deliberations, and that a transcript will be available to all jurors if there is any difficulty remembering the testimony. If you do take notes, all notes must be left each day in the jury room. Mr. Lopez will make sure that they are secure.

From this point until the time when you retire to deliberate, it is your duty not to discuss this case, and not to remain in the presence of other persons who may be discussing this case. In that regard, please remember that the parties and counsel in this case have been instructed to have no contact with any of you. So if you happen to see any of them outside this courtroom, and they do not acknowledge you, say hello, or make small talk, please do not take offense. As I mentioned earlier, they are not being rude — they are simply following my instructions.

Appendix F
Jury Instructions from Judge Christine M. Arguello (D. Colo.)

During the course of the trial you will receive all the evidence you legally may consider to decide the case. You, as jurors, must decide this case based solely on the evidence presented here within the four walls of this courtroom. This means that during the trial you must not conduct any independent research about this case, the matters in the case, and the individuals or corporations involved in the case, including the lawyers, the parties, and the witnesses. In other words, you should not consult dictionaries or reference materials, search the internet, websites, blogs, or use any other electronic tools to obtain information about this case or to help you decide the case. Please do not try to find out information from any source outside the confines of this courtroom. As I told you, until you retire to deliberate, you may not discuss this case with anyone, even your fellow jurors. After you retire to deliberate, you may begin discussing the case with your fellow jurors, but you cannot discuss the case with anyone else until you have returned a verdict and the case is at an end. I hope that for all of you this case is interesting and noteworthy.

I know that many of you use cell phones, Blackberries, the internet and other tools of technology. You may not, under any circumstances, have your cell phones, Blackberries, I-phones or the like on when court is in session or while you are deliberating. You also must not talk to anyone about this case or use these tools to communicate electronically with anyone about the case. This includes your family and friends. You may not communicate with anyone about the case on your cell phone, through e-mail, Blackberry, iPhone, text messaging, or on Twitter, through any blog or website, through any internet chat room, or by way of any other social networking websites, including Facebook, My Space, LinkedIn, and YouTube. Researching or gathering any information on your own that you think might be helpful is against the law and would be a violation of your oath.

Violation of this instruction could cause a mistrial, meaning all of our efforts over the course of the trial would have been wasted and we would have to start all over again with a new trial before a new jury. If you were to cause a mistrial by violating this order, you could be subject to paying all the costs of these proceedings and you could also be punished for contempt of court.

I wish I did not have to dwell on this topic, but this is not a trivial matter – in another case, after the evidence was completed, one juror, despite this order, "Googled" maps that she thought were relevant to the case. A mistrial was declared in that case and the juror faced contempt of court charges that could result in her being jailed and/or ordered to reimburse both the prosecution and the defense for costs and fees incurred in the trial. Her actions compromised a years-long investigation and prosecution, violated the defendant's right to know and confront all the evidence against him, and wasted all of the time expended by the Court, counsel, and her fellow jurors to hear the case.

Fairness to all concerned requires that all of us connected with this case deal with the information and with nothing other than the same information produced in this courtroom.

Appendix G
Jury Instructions from Judge Patrick J. Schiltz (D. Minn.)

F.

To ensure fairness, you jurors must obey the following rules:

First, do not talk among yourselves about this case, or about anyone involved with it, until the end of the trial when you go to the jury room to decide on your verdict.

Second, do not talk with anyone else about this case, or about anyone involved with it, until the trial has ended, and you have been discharged as jurors. This includes family members and friends. You may tell people that you are serving as a juror, but do not tell them anything else about the case.

I know that many of you use cell phones, iPhones, iPods, iPads, Androids, Blackberries, and other tools of technology. You must not use these devices to communicate electronically with anyone about this case, including your family and friends. That means that you must not call or text or email anyone about this case, and you must not use any blog or website to communicate about this case, including Facebook, Twitter, Google+, MySpace, LinkedIn, or YouTube. You must not use any other type of technology or social media, even if I have not specifically mentioned it. Please let me know immediately if you become aware that any juror has violated these instructions.

Third, when you are outside the courtroom, do not let anyone tell you anything about the case, or about anyone involved with it, until the trial has ended and your verdict has been accepted. If someone should try to talk to you about the case during the trial, please report it to me immediately.

Fourth, during the trial you should not talk with or speak to any of the parties, lawyers, or witnesses involved in this case. You should not even pass the time of day with any of them. It is important not only that you do justice in this case, but that you also give the appearance of doing justice. If a person from one side of the case sees you talking to a person from the other side — even if it is simply to comment on the weather — an unwarranted and unnecessary suspicion about your fairness might be aroused. If any lawyer, party, or witness does not speak to you when you pass in the hall, ride the elevator, or the like, remember it is because they are not supposed to talk with you either.

Fifth, do not read any news stories or articles about the case, or about anyone involved with it, or listen to any radio or television reports about the case or about anyone involved with it.

Sixth, do not do any research or make any investigation on your own about any matter involved in this case. You must decide this case based solely on the evidence presented here within the four walls of this courtroom. This means that, during the trial, you must not conduct any independent research about this case, the subject matter of this case, or the individuals or entities involved in this case. For example, you must not consult dictionaries or other reference materials; search the Internet, websites, or blogs; or use any other electronic tools to obtain information about this case or to help you decide this case. You must learn about this case only from the evidence that you receive here at the trial and from the law as I give it to you.

Seventh, during the trial, the lawyers and I will often be discussing legal and evidentiary matters before trial resumes in the morning, during the breaks, and after trial adjourns in the evening. You are not permitted to hear these discussions. Therefore, you should never enter the courtroom, except when I or a member of my staff bring you in as a group. And you should not talk to anyone who was present in the courtroom about what he or she may have seen or heard in the courtroom while you were absent.

Eighth, cell phones are not permitted in the jury room during deliberations. You may use cell phones in the jury room until you retire to deliberate on your verdict. During the trial, please leave your cell phones in the jury room or power them off before bringing them into the courtroom.

Ninth, do not make up your mind during the trial about what the verdict should be. Keep an open mind until after you have gone to the jury room to decide the case and you and your fellow jurors have discussed the evidence.

Appendix H
Jury Instructions from Judge John Joseph Tharp, Jr. (N.D. Ill.)

During your deliberations, you must not communicate with or provide any information to anyone by any means about this case. You many not use any electronic device or media, such as the telephone, a cell phone, smart phone, iPhone, Blackberry or computer, the Internet, any Internet service, any text or instant messaging service, any Internet chat room, blog, or website such as Facebook, MySpace, LinkedIn, YouTube or Twitter, to communicate to anyone any information about this case or to conduct any research about this case until I accept your verdict. In other words, you cannot talk to anyone on the phone, correspond with anyone, or electronically communicate with anyone about this case. You can only discuss the case in the jury room with your fellow jurors during deliberations.

You may not use these electronic means to investigate or communicate about the case because it is important that you decide this case based solely on the evidence presented in this courtroom. Information on the internet or available through social media might be wrong, incomplete, or inaccurate. You are only permitted to discuss the case with your fellow jurors during deliberations because they have seen and heard the same evidence you have. In our judicial system, it is important that you are not influenced by anything or anyone outside of this courtroom. Otherwise, your decision may be based on information known only by you and not your fellow jurors or the parties in the case. This would unfairly and adversely impact the judicial process.

Appendix I
Jury Instructions from Judge Benjamin H. Settle (W.D. Wash.)

INSTRUCTION NO. _____

I will now say a few words about your conduct as jurors.

First, keep an open mind throughout the trial, and do not decide what the verdict should be until you and your fellow jurors have completed your deliberations at the end of the case.

Second, because you must decide this case based only on the evidence received in the case and on my instructions as to the law that applies, you must not be exposed to any other information about the case or to the issues it involves during the course of your jury duty. Thus, until the end of the case or unless I tell you otherwise:

Do not communicate with anyone in any way and do not let anyone else communicate with you in any way about the merits of the case or anything to do with it. This includes discussing the case in person, in writing, by phone or electronic means, via email, text messaging, or any Internet chat room, blog, website or other feature. This applies to communicating with your fellow jurors until I give you the case for deliberation, and it applies to communicating with everyone else including your family members, your employer, the media or press, and the people involved in the trial, although you may notify your family and your employer that you have been seated as a juror in the case. But, if you are asked or approached in any way about your jury service or anything about this case, you must respond that you have been ordered not to discuss the matter and to report the contact to the court.

Because you will receive all the evidence and legal instruction you properly may consider to return a verdict: do not read, watch, or listen to any news or media accounts or commentary about the case or anything to do with it; do not do any research, such as consulting dictionaries, searching the Internet or using other reference materials; and do not make any investigation or in any other way try to learn about the case on your own.

The law requires these restrictions to ensure the parties have a fair trial based on the same evidence that each party has had an opportunity to address. A juror who violates these restrictions jeopardizes the fairness of these proceedings, and a mistrial could result that would require the entire trial process to start over. If any juror is exposed to any outside information, please notify the court immediately.

Appendix J
Jury Instructions for Judge James Boasberg (D.D.C.)

UNITED STATES DISTRICT COURT
FOR THE DISTRICT OF COLUMBIA

<u>PRELIMINARY INSTRUCTIONS</u>

<u>Discussion of Case</u>

You are not permitted to discuss this case with anyone until this case is submitted to you for your decision at the end of my final instructions. This means that, until the case is submitted to you, you may not talk about it even with your fellow jurors. This is because we don't want you making decisions until you've heard all the evidence and the instructions of law. In addition, you may not talk about the case with anyone else. It should go without saying that you also may not write about the case electronically through any blog, posting, or other communication, including "social networking" sites such as Facebook or Twitter until you have delivered your verdict and the case is over. This is because you must decide the case based on what happens here in the courtroom, not on what someone may or may not tell you outside the courtroom. I'm sure that, when we take our first recess, you will call home or work and tell them you have been selected for a jury. They will undoubtedly ask what kind of case you're sitting on. You may tell them it is a civil case, but nothing else. Now, when the case is over, you may discuss any part of it with anyone you wish, but until then, you may not do so.

Although it is a natural human tendency to talk with people with whom you may come into contact, you must not talk to any of the parties, their attorneys, or any witnesses in this case during the time you serve on this jury. If you encounter anyone connected with the case outside the courtroom, you should avoid having any conversation with them, overhearing their conversation, or having any contact with them at all. For example, if you find yourself in a courthouse corridor, elevator, or any other location where the case is being discussed by attorneys, parties, witnesses, or anyone else, you should immediately leave the area to avoid hearing such discussions. If you do overhear a discussion about the case, you should report that to me as soon as you can. Finally, if you see any of the attorneys or witnesses involved in the case and they turn and walk away from you, they are not being rude; they are merely following the same instruction that I gave to them.

It is very unlikely, but if someone tries to talk to you about the case, you should refuse to do so and immediately let me know by telling the courtroom deputy. Don't tell the other jurors; just let me know, and I'll bring you in to discuss it.

Because you must decide this case based only on what occurs in the courtroom, you may not conduct any independent investigation of the law or the facts in the case. That used to mean that you could not conduct any research in books or newspapers or visit the scene of the alleged offense. In this electronic age, it also means you cannot conduct any other kind of research--for example, researching any issue on the internet, asking any questions of anyone via email or text, or otherwise communicating about or investigating the facts or law connected to the case.

I want to explain a bit further why there is a ban on internet communications and research concerning the case. Unfortunately courts around the country have occasionally experienced problems with jurors ignoring this rule, sometimes resulting in costly retrials. Generally speaking, these jurors have not sought to corrupt the process, rather they have been seeking additional information to aid them in what is undoubtedly a heavy and solemn responsibility. Nonetheless, there are sound reasons for this rule.

In the first place, obviously, not everything one sees on line is true. This includes not only persons responding to whatever postings you may make about the case, but also can involve established websites. For example, a mapping site might not reflect the way a location appeared at the times that are at issue in the case. Furthermore, even items that are technically true can change their meaning and significance based upon context.

Both sides are entitled to have the chance to not only dispute or rebut evidence presented by the other side, but also to argue to you how that evidence should be considered within the factual and legal confines of the case. Any secret communications or research by you robs them of those opportunities and can distort the process, sometimes with negative results. It is for those reasons, that I instruct you that you should not use the internet to communicate about the case or do any research about the case.

Finally, we have a fine court reporter here taking down testimony, but you will not have a transcript with you during deliberations. You must rely on your memory and, if you take them, your notes as an aid to that memory. So I ask you to pay close attention, and we will begin with the opening statement by the government.

Appendix K
Jury Instructions from Judge Herman J. Weber (S.D. Ohio)

CLOSING REMARKS

Nothing that I have said in these instructions and nothing in the manner in which the Special Verdicts have been prepared or explained to you is intended to suggest or convey in any way a result I think you should reach as this is the exclusive duty and responsibility of the jury. I state to you categorically that the Court has no opinion as to the disputed facts of this case or the propriety of any verdict you may return.

I cannot embody all the law in any single part of these instructions. In considering one portion, you must consider it in the light of and in harmony with all the instructions.

I have instructed you on all the law necessary for your deliberations. Whether certain instructions are applicable may depend upon the conclusions you reach on the facts.

It is your duty, as jurors, to confer with one another and to deliberate with a view to reaching an agreement, if you can do so without doing violence to your individual judgment. Each of you must decide the case for yourself, but do so only after an impartial consideration of all the legal evidence in the case with other jurors. In the course of your deliberations, do not hesitate to re-examine your own views and change your opinion, if you are convinced it is erroneous.

Do not surrender your honest conclusion as to weight or effect of the legal evidence, however, solely because of the opinion of other jurors, or for the mere purpose of returning a verdict.

Remember always that you are not partisans. You are judges--impartial triers of the facts. Your sole interest is to ascertain the truth from the legal evidence in the case. Do not take a firm position at the outset and then be too proud to change your position if you become convinced that your position is wrong.

You must not be influenced by any consideration of sympathy or prejudice. It is your duty to carefully weigh the legal evidence, to decide all disputed questions of fact, to apply these instructions to your findings, and to render your verdict accordingly. In fulfilling your duty, your efforts must be to arrive at a just verdict. Consider the legal evidence and make your findings with intelligence and impartiality, and without bias, sympathy or prejudice, so that the litigants will feel that their case was fairly and impartially tried. If, during the course of the trial, I said or did anything which you consider an indication of my view on any disputed fact, you are instructed to disregard it because only you, the Jury, determine such matters.

If during your deliberations you wish to communicate with me, please put your communication in writing and give it to the Courtroom Deputy, who will deliver it to me.

The Court will place in your possession the exhibits, the Special Verdicts and a copy of these instructions.

Upon retiring to the jury room, you will select one of you to act as your foreperson. The foreperson will retain possession of these records and return them to the courtroom. The foreperson will see that your discussions are orderly and that each juror has the opportunity to discuss the case and to cast his or her vote; otherwise, the authority of the foreperson is the same as any other juror.

Until your verdict is announced in open court, you are not to disclose to anyone else the status of your deliberations or the nature of your verdict. When you arrive at a unanimous verdict - that is whenever all of you agree upon a verdict - you will sign the Special Verdicts in ink and notify the Courtroom Deputy. You will then be returned to the courtroom.

Appendix L
Jury Instructions for Judge Dora L. Irizarry (E.D.N.Y.)

UNITED STATES DISTRICT COURT
EASTERN DISTRICT OF NEW YORK

PART THREE

And now for the third part of the charge – the closing instructions. Let me say a few words about your deliberations.

Keep in mind that nothing I have said in these instructions is intended to suggest to you in any way what I think your verdict should be. That is entirely for you to decide. In order that your deliberations may proceed in an orderly fashion, you must have a foreperson, but of course the foreperson's vote is not entitled to any greater weight than that of any other juror. Traditionally, the first juror chosen is the foreperson. That is Juror # 1.

Your function, to reach a fair and impartial verdict from the law and the evidence, is an important one. Your verdict must be unanimous.

When you return to the jury room, you must discuss the case. It is the duty of each of you to consult with your fellow jurors and to deliberate with a view toward reaching agreement on a verdict, if you can do so without violating your individual judgment and your conscience. In the course of your deliberations, no one should surrender conscientious beliefs of what the truth is and what the weight and effect of the evidence is. Moreover, you must each decide the case for yourself and not merely acquiesce in the conclusion of your fellow jurors. Nevertheless, I do ask you to examine the issues and the evidence before you with candor and frankness and a proper deference to and regard for the opinions of one another. Do not hesitate to change your opinions if you are convinced they are wrong. Remember that the parties and the court are relying upon you to give full and conscientious deliberation and consideration to the issues and evidence before you. By so doing, you carry out to the fullest your oaths as jurors: to well and truly try the issues of this case and a true verdict render.

Remember also that your verdict must be based solely on the evidence in the case and the law as the court has given it to you, not on anything else. You must not be influenced by any assumptions, conjectures, sympathy, bias, prejudice, or inferences not warranted by the facts.

The question of possible punishment of the defendant is of no concern to the jury and, pursuant to your oath as jurors, you cannot allow consideration of the punishment that may be imposed upon the defendant, if convicted, to enter into or influence your deliberations in any sense or manner. The duty of imposing sentence rests exclusively upon the court. Your function is to weigh the evidence in the case and to determine whether or not the defendant is guilty beyond a reasonable doubt, based solely on the evidence.

Bear in mind that the government has the burden of proof at all times and that you must be convinced of the defendant's guilt beyond a reasonable doubt as to each and every element of each offense charged in order to return a guilty verdict as to that offense. If you find that this burden has not been met, you must return a verdict of not guilty.

During your deliberations, you must not communicate with or provide any information to anyone by any means about this case. You may not use any electronic device or media, such as a telephone, cell phone, smart phone, iPhone, Blackberry or computer, the internet, any internet service, any text or instant messaging service, any internet chat room, blog, or website such as Facebook, MySpace, LinkedIn, YouTube or Twitter, to communicate to anyone any information about this case or to conduct any research about this case until after I accept your verdict.

Additionally, it is very important that you not communicate with anyone outside the jury room about your deliberations or about anything at all concerning this case. Indeed, the jury must deliberate **only** when all twelve jurors are present inside the jury room and no one else is present. You must not discuss the case outside of the jury room, even if all twelve jurors are together, such as in the court corridor. There is only one exception to this rule. If it becomes necessary during your deliberations to communicate with me for any reason, simply send a note through the Marshal, noting the date and time and signed by your foreperson or by one or more members of the jury, **utilizing only the juror numbers you were given corresponding to your seat in the courtroom. Please do not sign your names.** No member of the jury should ever attempt to communicate with me except by a signed writing, and I will never communicate with any member of the jury on any subject touching the merits of the case other than in writing, or orally here in open court. If you send any notes to the court, do not disclose anything about your deliberations. **Specifically, do not disclose to anyone – not even to me – how the jury stands, numerically or otherwise, on the question of guilt or non-guilt of the defendant, until after you have reached a unanimous verdict or have been discharged.**

When you have reached a decision, please have the foreperson sign the verdict form as **Juror #1** and put the date and time on it and notify the Marshal by note that you have reached a verdict. I remind you that **any verdict you reach must be unanimous.**

As I have told you throughout the trial, if you wish to review any portion of the testimony, you may simply indicate that in a note. In order to assist us in quickly locating the testimony you wish to review, please be as specific as possible when making your request. Please let us know what part of the testimony of a specific witness you want review, and please be patient while we find it in the record. If you need clarification of or further instruction on any point of law, you should indicate that in a note to the court. Four copies of these final instructions will be provided to you when you retire to your deliberations for your reference. If you wish to see any of the exhibits received in evidence, you may request those as well and they will either be sent into the jury room or made available for your inspection in the courtroom.

Your oath sums up your duty – and that is – without fear or favor to any person, you will well and truly try the issues in this case according to the evidence given to you in court and the laws of the United States.

Before asking you to retire and begin your deliberations, let me first consult with counsel to be certain I have not overlooked any point.

You may now retire to your deliberations.

Dated: Brooklyn, New York
      May 25, 2011

Appendix M
Jury Instructions from Judge Benita Y. Pearson (N.D. Ohio)

ADMONITION

1. ADMONITION. It is now my duty to give you what is called "The Admonition". This is a standing court order that applies throughout the trial. I will try to remind you of The Admonition at every recess, but even if I forget to remind you, it still applies.

Ladies and gentlemen, you have been selected as jurors in this case. We have taken the time to seat a neutral jury so this case can be decided based just on what goes on in the courtroom, and not on outside influences. You are required to decide this case based solely on the evidence that is presented to you in this courtroom. It is my role as the judge to determine what evidence is admissible and what is not admissible. It would be a violation of your duties, and unfair to the parties, if you should obtain other information about the case, which might be information that is not admissible as evidence.

You must carefully listen to all the evidence, and evaluate all of it. Do not reach any conclusions until you have heard all the evidence, the arguments of the attorneys, and the judge's instructions of law. Otherwise you will have an incomplete picture of the case.

Do not discuss this case among yourselves or with anyone else. The reason for this is you might be given information or an opinion that could alter the way in which you view the evidence or the instructions or even how the case should come out. Such an opinion or conclusion would be based on an incomplete or inaccurate view of the evidence and therefore would be clearly unfair.

2. WARNING ON OUTSIDE INFORMATION. In addition, you absolutely must not try to get information from any other source. The ban on sources outside the courtroom applies to information from all sources such as family, friends, the Internet, reference books, newspapers, magazines, television, radio, a computer, a Blackberry, iPhone, smart phone, and any other electronic device. This ban on outside information also includes any personal investigation, including visiting the site, looking into news accounts, talking to possible witnesses, re-enacting the allegations in the (Complaint)(Indictment), or any other act that would otherwise affect the fairness and impartiality that you must have as juror.

3. WARNING ON OUTSIDE INFLUENCE. The effort to exclude misleading outside influences information also puts a limit on getting legal information from television entertainment. This would apply to popular TV shows such as Law and Order, Boston Legal, Judge Judy, older shows like L.A. Law, Perry Mason, or Matlock, and any other fictional show dealing with the legal system. In addition, this would apply to shows such as CSI and NCIS, which present the use of scientific procedures to resolve criminal investigations. These and other similar shows may leave you with an improper preconceived idea about the legal system. As far as this case is concerned, you are not prohibited from watching such shows. However, there are many reasons why you cannot rely on TV legal programs, including the fact that these shows: (1) are not subject to the rules of evidence and legal safeguards that apply in this courtroom, and (2) are works of fiction that present unrealistic situations for dramatic effect. While entertaining, TV legal drams condense, distort, or even ignore many procedures that take place in real cases and real courtrooms. No matter how convincing they try to be, these shows simply cannot depict the reality of an actual trial or investigation. You must put aside anything you think you know about the legal system that you saw on TV.

4. WARNING ON OUTSIDE CONTACT. Finally, you must not have contact with anyone about this case, other than the judge and court employees. This includes sending or receiving email, Twitter, text messages or similar updates, using blogs and chat rooms, and the use of Facebook, MySpace, LinkedIn, and other social media sites of any kind regarding this case or any aspect of your jury service during the trial. If anyone tries to contact you about the case, directly or indirectly, do not allow that person to have contact with you. If any person persists in contacting you or speaking with you, that could be jury tampering, which is a very serious crime. If anyone contacts you in this manner, report this to my courtroom deputy as quickly as possible.

5. CONCLUSION. You should know that if this Admonition is violated, there could be a mistrial. A mistrial means that the case is stopped before it is finished and must be retried at a later date. This can lead to a great deal of expense for the parties and for the taxpayers, namely you and your neighbors. No one wants to see money, especially tax dollars, wasted. If a mistrial were to be declared based on a violation of this Admonition, the juror responsible could be required to pay the cost of the first trial, and could also be punished for contempt of court.

Appendix N
Jury Instructions from Judge Dan A. Polster (N.D. Ohio)

Proposed Model Jury Instructions
The Use of Electronic Technology to Conduct Research on
or Communicate about a Case

Prepared by the Judicial Conference Committee on
Court Administration and Case Management
December 2009

Before Trial:

You, as jurors, must decide this case based solely on the evidence presented here within the four walls of this courtroom. This means that during the trial you must not conduct any independent research about this case, the matters in the case, and the individuals or corporations involved in the case. In other words, you should not consult dictionaries or reference materials, search the internet, websites, blogs, or use any other electronic tools to obtain information about this case or to help you decide the case. Please do not try to find out information from any source outside the confines of this courtroom.

Until you retire to deliberate, you may not discuss this case with anyone, even your fellow jurors. After you retire to deliberate, you may begin discussing the case with your fellow jurors, but you cannot discuss the case with anyone else until you have returned a verdict and the case is at an end. I hope that for all of you this case is interesting and noteworthy. I know that many of you use cell phones, Blackberries, the internet and other tools of technology. You also must not talk to anyone about this case or use these tools to communicate electronically with anyone about the case. This includes your family and friends. You may not communicate with anyone about the case on your cell phone, through e-mail, Blackberry, iPhone, text messaging, or on Twitter, through any blog or website, through any internet chat room, or by way of any other social networking websites, including Facebook, My Space, LinkedIn, and YouTube.

At the Close of the Case:

During your deliberations, you must not communicate with or provide any information to anyone by any means about this case. You may not use any electronic device or media, such as a telephone, cell phone, smart phone, iPhone, Blackberry or computer; the internet, any internet service, or any text or instant messaging service; or any internet chat room, blog, or website such as Facebook, My Space, LinkedIn, YouTube or Twitter, to communicate to anyone any information about this case or to conduct any research about this case until I accept your verdict.

Appendix O
Jury Instructions from Judge John T. Fowlkes, Jr. (W.D. Tenn.)

PRELIMINARY INSTRUCTIONS

My responsibilities as the judge in this trial are to make sure that the trial is run fairly and efficiently, to make decisions about evidence and to instruct you about the law that applies to this case. You must take the law as I give it to you even if you personally disagree with it. Nothing I say is meant to reflect my own opinion about the facts of the case. As jurors, you are the ones that will decide this case.

Your responsibility as jurors is to decide what the facts of the case are. This is your job, and no one else's. You must think about all the evidence and all the testimony and then decide what each piece of evidence means and how important you think that it is. This includes how much you believe what each of the witnesses said. What you decide about any fact in this case is final.

When it is time for you to decide the case, you are only allowed to consider the evidence that was admitted in the case. Evidence includes only the sworn testimony of witnesses, the exhibits admitted into evidence, and anything else I tell you to consider as evidence.

The questions the lawyers ask the witnesses are not evidence. Only the answers are evidence. You should not think that something is true just because one of the lawyers asks questions that assume or suggest that it is.

I may ask some of the witnesses questions myself. These questions are not meant to reflect my opinion about the evidence. If I ask questions, my only reason would be to ask about things that may not have been fully explored.

During the trial the lawyers may object to certain questions or statements made by the other lawyers or witnesses. I will rule on these objections according to the law. My rulings for or against one side or the other are not meant to reflect my opinions about the facts of the case.

Possible penalty should not influence your decision. It is the duty of the judge to fix the penalty within the limits provided by law.

You must not discuss the case with anyone, including your family or friends. You must not even discuss it with the other jurors until the time comes for you to decide the case. When it is time for you to decide the case, I will send you to the jury room. Then you should discuss the case among yourselves, but only in the jury room and only when all the jurors are there. When the trial is over, you may, if you wish, discuss the case with anyone.

If I call for a recess during the trial, I will either send you back to the jury room or allow you to leave the courtroom on your own and go about your business. But you must not discuss the case with anyone or let anyone discuss it with you or in your presence. If someone tries to do that, tell him or her to stop, and explain that as a juror you are not allowed to discuss the case. If he or she continues, leave and report the incident one of the court security officers or to me as soon as you return to court, and it will be dealt with.

You must not talk to the defendant, the lawyers, or the witnesses about anything at all, even if it has nothing to do with the case.

It is very important that you only get information about the case in court, when you are acting as the jury and when the defendant, the lawyers, and I are all here.

During the course of the trial, you will receive all of the evidence you may properly consider to decide the case. Because of this, you shall not attempt to do any research on your own or gather any information on your own that you think might be helpful. Do not engage in any outside reading or internet investigation, or visit any places mentioned in the case, or try to learn about the case outside of the courtroom in any other manner.

I do not know whether there will be any media reports in the newspapers, on TV, or on the radio about this particular case. However, out of an abundance of caution, I am directing you that while you are serving on this case, you will not watch or listen to any local news. You, as jurors, must base your decision solely on the evidence and law you hear in the courtroom.

After all the evidence has been presented and after the lawyers have given their arguments, I will give you detailed instructions about the rules of law that apply in this case. You should consider all of my instructions as a connected series. Taken all together, they are the law you must follow. After receiving the instructions of law, you will go to the jury room to decide on your verdict. Your verdict must be unanimous. That means that every juror must agree on it, and it must reflect the individual decision of each juror.

It is important for you to keep an open mind and not make a decision about anything in the case until you go to the jury room to decide the case.

The law presumes that the defendant is innocent of the charges against him, therefore, you as the jury, must enter upon this investigation with the presumption that the defendant is not guilty of any crime and this presumption stays with the defendant unless it is rebutted and overturned by competent and credible proof. It is, therefore, incumbent upon the government, before you can convict the defendant, to establish to your satisfaction, beyond a reasonable doubt, that the crime charged in the indictment has been committed; that the same was committed within Western District of Tennessee, before the indictment was returned and that the defendant on trial committed the crime in such manner that would make him guilty under the law as it has been defined and explained to you.

The government has the burden of proving the guilt of the defendant beyond a reasonable doubt, and this burden never shifts but it remains on the government throughout the trial of the case. The defendant is not required to prove his innocence. The government must have proven beyond a reasonable doubt all of the elements of the crime charged and that it was committed before the finding and returning of the indictment in this case.

While the government's burden of proof is a strict or heavy burden, it is not necessary that a defendant's guilt be proved beyond all possible doubt. It is only required that the government's proof exclude any "reasonable doubt".

A "reasonable doubt" is a real doubt, based upon reason and common sense after careful and impartial consideration of all the evidence in the case. Proof beyond a reasonable doubt, therefore, is proof of such a convincing character that you would be willing to rely and act upon it without hesitation in the most important of your own affairs.

It is your job to decide what the facts of this case are. You must decide which witnesses you believe and how important you think their testimony is. You do not have to accept or reject everything a witness said. You are free to believe all, none, or any part of any person's testimony.

In deciding which testimony you believe, you should rely on your own common sense and everyday experience. There is no fixed set of rules for judging whether you believe a witness, but it may help you to think about these questions:

(1)   Was the witness able to see or hear clearly?

            How long was the witness watching or listening?

            Was anything else going on that might have distracted the witness?

(2)   Did the witness seem to have a good memory?

(3)   How did the witness look and act while testifying? Did the witness seem to be making an honest effort to tell the truth, or did the witness seem to evade the questions?

(4)   Has there been any evidence presented regarding the witness' intelligence, respectability or reputation for truthfulness?

(5)   Does the witness have any bias, prejudice, or personal interest in how the case is decided?

(6)   Have there been any promises, threats, suggestions, or other influences that may have affected how the witness testified?

(7)   In general, does the witness have any special reason to tell the truth, or any special reason to swear to a falsehood?

(8)   All in all, how reasonable does the witness's testimony seem when you think about all the other evidence in the case?

Sometimes the testimony of different witnesses will not agree, and you must decide which testimony you accept. You should think about whether the disagreement involves something important or not, and whether you think someone is lying or is simply mistaken. People see and hear things differently, and witnesses may testify honestly but simply be wrong about what they thought they saw or remembered. It is also a good idea to think about which testimony agrees best with the other evidence in the case.

However, you may conclude that a witness deliberately lied about something that is important to how you decide the case. If so, you may choose not to accept anything that witness said. On the other hand, if you think the witness lied about some things but told the truth about others, you may simply accept the part you think is true and ignore the rest.

Some of you might have heard the terms "circumstantial evidence" and "direct evidence." These are the two basic types of evidence that exist in law. Direct evidence is direct proof of a fact, such as the testimony of an eyewitness. Circumstantial evidence is proof of facts from which you may infer or conclude that other facts exist. I will give you further instructions on these as well as other matters at the end of the case. The Court instructs that you may consider both kinds of evidence, which are considered to be of equal value in the law.

The defendant is charged in Count One and Count Two of the indictment with conspiracy to commit the crime of possession with the intent to distribute a controlled substance in violation of federal law. A conspiracy is a kind of criminal partnership. For you to find the defendant guilty of the conspiracy charge, the government must prove the following elements beyond a reasonable doubt:

(A)   First, that two or more persons conspired, or agreed, to commit the crime of possession with the intent to distribute a controlled substance; and

(B)   Second, that the defendant knowingly and voluntarily joined the conspiracy.

Again, I will give you more detailed instructions about conspiracy at the end of the case.

The Court will not provide you with a transcript of the testimony at the end of the trial. Therefore, you must listen very carefully to the testimony. Each of you will be allowed to take notes during the trial for your own use during your deliberations. You are not required to take notes. Independent memory can be as precise as written notes. You will be provided with notebooks and pens should you decide to take notes.

Remember, you can have no sympathy or prejudice or allow anything but the law and evidence to have any influence upon your verdict, and you must render your verdict with absolute fairness and impartiality.

This completes my opening instructions. Now, we will proceed with reading the indictment.

Appendix P
Jury Instructions from Judge James C. Dever III (E.D.N.C.)

Please remember YOU WILL BE A JUDGE. You will be the judges of the facts. And it is imperative that you not to talk about that case to anyone, even your fellow jurors, before all of the evidence has been received and you have retired to your jury room to determine your verdict.

You must not read about the case in the newspaper or look at or listen to reports about it on radio or television. You must not attempt to research or investigate this case, the matters at issue, and the persons involved. In other words, you should not consult dictionaries, reference materials or the like, nor should you engage in internet searches, access websites, refer to blogs, or use any tool, electronic or otherwise, to obtain or post information about the case. You will decide the case based on the information presented in this room, and you will not communicate in any way about it before your begin your deliberations.

So until you retire to deliberate, you may not discuss this case with anyone. You may not speak nor may you write about your work as jurors or about the case, through any means. I know that many of you use cell phones, the internet, and other tools of technology as a means of communication. Phones, e-mail, text messaging, blogs, websites, internet chat rooms, twitter, and other social and professional networking sites, like Facebook, My Space, LinkedIn, and YouTube, now are the stuff of daily life for many. But these are not avenues you can use to share about your work as a juror or this case.

This is very important. The parties are entitled to have you determine the case based solely on evidence that you all hear together in the courtroom, and on the arguments of the attorneys and my charge as to the law, given to each of you.

Appendix Q
Jury Instructions from Judge Donald C. Pogue (Ct. of Int'l Trade)

Conduct of the jury

Now, a few words about your conduct as jurors.

First, during the trial you are not to discuss the case with anyone or allow anyone to discuss it with you. This includes family and persons living in your household, friends and co-workers, spiritual leaders, advisors, or therapists.

Until you go to the jury room at the end of the trial to deliberate on your verdict, you simply are not to talk about this case, even with your fellow jurors. This means no discussion with anyone, anytime, anywhere – not in the elevators, not in the halls, nowhere. You may say you are on a jury and how long the trial may take, but that is all. This is necessary to preserve the integrity of your decision-making as a jury.

After you retire to deliberate, you may begin discussing the case with your fellow jurors, but you cannot discuss the case with anyone else until you have returned a verdict and the case is at an end.

I know that many of you use iPhones, other smartphones, the internet and tools of technology and social media. Just as you must not talk to anyone about this case, until I accept your verdict, you also must not use any electronic devices or any social media, including, for example, Facebook or Twitter, to communicate any information about this case to anyone including your family and friends. Again, you may say you are on a jury and how long the trial may take, but that is all. And you must not use any device to record or to share with anyone what goes on during this trial. If you see another juror doing anything that I have told you not to do, you must tell me right away.

Once the trial is over and I have released you from jury duty, you may discuss the case with anyone, but you are not required to do so. Do any of you have any questions about this that you wish to ask?

Second, do not read or listen to anything touching on this case in any way. If *anyone* tries to talk to you about it, you must bring it to the court's attention right away. This includes attorneys, witnesses, and parties in this case.

Third, do not try to do any research or make any investigation about the case on your own or as a group. Do not use dictionaries, the Internet, or other reference materials. Do not investigate the case or conduct any experiments. Do not contact anyone to assist you, such as a family accountant, doctor, or lawyer.

Fourth, pay close attention to the evidence that is presented in this trial. Justice will be served only if each of you gives the evidence your full attention and consideration.

Finally, do not form any opinion until all the evidence is in. Keep an open mind until you start your deliberations together at the end of the case.

It is my practice to instruct jurors not to take notes during the trial. So please do not take notes. I give you this instruction because in my experience it is difficult to take detailed notes and pay attention to what the witnesses are saying at the same time. And it is your attention that is vital. In addition, we depend on the judgment of all members of the jury; you all must remember the evidence in this case. After the trial, during your deliberations, you may ask to look at any of the exhibits or to have the transcript of testimony read back to you. In that way, if you need to refresh your memory of the trial and the evidence you have seen, you will be able to do so.

Appendix R
Jury Oath from Judge Barbara M.G. Lynn (N.D. Tex.)

Do each of you solemnly swear or affirm that you will follow the Court's instructions, which are that until the case is over, you will not access in any way the news about this case, either by the Internet, by print media, by radio, or by television, and that you will not communicate with any others about this case – this includes not talking about it by person or by phone, not writing, blogging or tweeting about it, and not using any social networking sites, examples of which are Facebook, MySpace, LinkedIn, and Twitter, to discuss or work any aspect of this case or your work as a juror?

If you agree, please say I do.

www.ingramcontent.com/pod-product-compliance
Lightning Source LLC
Chambersburg PA
CBHW080610290526
45790CB00007B/2716